FOLK DANCES

Bihu (Assam)

Bhangra (Punjab)

Dandiya Ras (Gujarat)

Dhumal (Kashmir)

Cheraw (Mizoram)

Jatra & Baul (West Bengal)

Nicobarese dance
(Andaman and Nicobar)

Garba (Gujarat)

Ghoomar (Rajasthan)

Dhamal dance (Haryana)

Naga dance (Nagaland)

Singhi Chham (Sikkim)

Taranghmel (Goa)

Dollu Kunitha (Karnataka)

Kinnauri Nati (Himachal Pradesh)

This Book:

Dance is a performing art that becomes a prime source of expressing happiness on any occasion, transcending all barriers of culture and development. India is a nation with diverse cultures and languages. Dance and music have played a remarkable role in unification and in bringing about integration of different castes and communities in the country. Using the body as a means of communication, dance is easily the most understood art form.

Ages ago dance, as a structured entity, was essentially a part of the devotional process. This becomes particularly evident when one studies the old temples in any corner of India. Statues, pillars, frescoes and paintings abound in temples, pillars and caves abound with female as well as male dancers dancing and playing instruments with people watching the performance. When combined with song and story-telling, dance metamorphosed into theatre. One aspect or other predominates in the theatre and the performing arts as we accept them today.

The *Natya Shastra* is the earliest Indian text on the subject and it speaks of *ekaharya* (solo dance) and the *anekaharya* (dance as performed by more than one person). Written by Sage Bharata, the work divides dance into *nritta*, i.e. pure dance and *nritya*, i.e. expressional dance or pantomime. While the former is an act of beauty not seeking to convey any meaning, the latter depicts emotions through facial expressions, movements of the eyes and stylised gestures of the hands called *mudras* or *hastas*. *Nritta* and *nritya* exist hand in hand. The latter refers to enactments of stories and concepts, through verse (*sahitya*), hand movements (*hastas*), and facial expressions (*abhinaya*). The mode is in two temperaments: *tandava* or the vigorous masculine movements represent the male principle symbolised by Lord Shiva, as in Kathakali, and *lasya* or the feminine principle symbolised by Goddess Parvati, consort of Lord Shiva, for example in Bharatanatyam and Manipuri. Kathak is the only dance form that encompasses both.

Dance is a physical and visual art form that has an immediate and massive impact on the onlooker. The various Indian forms act like a window to India's rich cultural heritage. Dance is a form of art, where the body is used as a medium of communication. Indian dances have influenced several other realms of art like poetry, sculpture, architecture, literature, music and theatre. The earliest archaeological evidence is a beautiful statuette of a dancing girl dated around 6000 BC. This was found at Mohenjodaro during archaeological excavations.

The four original classical dances are Bharatanatyam, Kathak, Kathakali and Manipuri. It was much later that Kuchipudi and Odissi joined this hallowed category. All six of these forms have their roots in the *Natya Shastra* and the *Natayaveda*. While Bharatanatyam has been popularised by dancers like Balasaraswati, Indrani Rehman, Padma Subramanyam and many others, the very name of Kathak reminds one of Birju Maharaj followed by Shovana Narayan and Uma Sharama. While Manipuri has gained popularity particularly due to the efforts of Singhajit and Charu Mathur, Kuchipudi and the names of Raja and Radha Reddy have become synonymous. Dancers like Sanjukata Panigrahi and Sonal Mansingh have done a lot to keep alive the tradition of Odissi.

———— •◆• ————

Let's know
DANCES
OF INDIA

Aakriti Sinha

Sinha, Aakriti
Let's know DANCES OF INDIA
Star, New Delhi 2006

© Star Publications Pvt. Ltd., 2006
ISBN 81-7650-097-6

First Edition : 2006
Price : Rs. 225/-
     (in U.K. £ 8.95)

Published in India by
STAR PUBLICATIONS PVT. LTD.
4/5-B, Asaf Ali Road
New Delhi-110 002
(e-mail: starpub@vsnl.net)

Distributors in the U.K.:
INDIAN BOOK SHELF
55, Warren Street., London W1T 5NW
Tel : 020 - 7380 0622, E-mail : indbooks@aol.com

Prepress Artworks
Jupiter, New Delhi-110 001 (India)
E-mail : jupiteradvtg@yahoo.com

Printed at: Everest Press, Okhla-II, New Delhi

Acknowledgement

The author and publishers of this book express their gratitude to Ms Manju Gupta who contributed her skills by reviewing and editing the script, and making it a pride publication.

Our thanks are also due to Ms Sangeet Gandhi, Ms Nandita Singh and all those whose photographic contributions have supplemented the text and made the book more attractive.

CONTENTS

The Dance Tradition of India

Dance is a primeval expression of joy and serves as a means of communication, transcending all barriers of culture. Dance created through rhythmic movements is very sensuous and the feeling of bliss it evokes is very spiritual. Ancient men were probably mimicking the movements of birds and animals to depict their unconscious grace and freedom of movement. Dance essentially began as a part of the devotional process. Gradually, dance combined with song and story-telling, metamorphosed into a performing art.

Dance in India is believed to have originated with Brahma, the creator, who was asked to create a pastime for the gods. So he took *pathya* (words) from the *Rigveda, abhinaya* (gestures) from the *Yajurveda, geet* (music and chant) from *Samaveda* and *rasa* (sentiment and emotions) from *Atharvaveda,* to form the fifth *Veda* called the *Natyaveda.* When Lord Shiva danced, the gods gathered around and played instruments or sang. Thus Shiva came to be known as Nataraja. If Shiva danced in joy, the dance was known as *ananda tandava* and if in anger, it was called *roudra tandava.* This art of *natya* was conveyed to sage Bharata who wrote the **Natya Shastra** to record it all. This treatise explains the intricacies of dance including the *mudras* or hand formations and their meanings, kinds of emotions and their categorisation including the types of attire, the stage, the ornaments and even the audience.

In ancient times, the temple was the centre of activity in the village where dance was performed on a regular basis before the presiding diety as a form of devotion. Since there were no halls, clubs or theatres as we have today, dancers performed in the temples. The dancers lived in the temple land and were employed by the temple. Gradually the dancers moved from the temples to homes of the rich landowners and royalty who could afford to have the dancer perform for them exclusively. The charm of special dance performances gradually got lost as larger audiences were not able to see the dance. Today we have **classical** as well as **folk dances** that have emerged from the roots of Indian traditions based upon our epics and mythology.

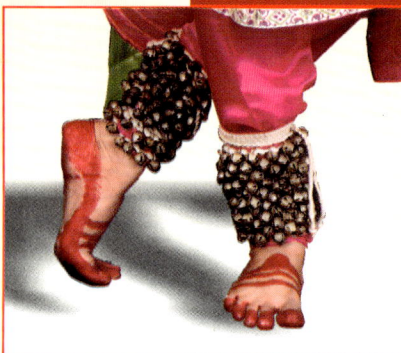

Elements of Classical Dance

An Introduction:

There are some common elements in various dance forms of India, no matter from which region they originate.

Abhinaya is common to all classical dances. It is the expression in dance or *nritya*. It is the art of telling a story through *hastas* or gestures, movement and facial expressions. In contrast, *nritta* signifies pure expressional meaning and symbolism. It is a movement that has beauty but does not tell a story. *Abhinaya* has been categorised in the **Natya Shastra** into four types:

- *Angika* or physical where every part of the body is used to convey a meaning with *hasta mudras* (hand gestures), *mandis* (postures) and even the walk of the dancer.

- *Vachikabhinaya* is the vocal/verbal aspect as used today by members of the orchestra or the supporting non-dancing cast.

- *Aharyabhinaya* or external expression, mood and background as conveyed by costume, make-up, accessories and sets.

- *Satvikabhinaya* or psychological expression as shown by the eyes in particular and as a whole by the entire being of the performer, who feels the mood, the character and the emotion as emanating from the self, not as an act or practical presentation.

All dance forms revolve around the nine *rasas* or emotions: *shringar* (love), *hasya* (happiness), *krodha* (anger), *bhibasta* (disdain or revulsion), *bhaya* (fear), *veerata* (courage), *karuna* (compassion), *adbhuta* (wonder) and *shanta* (serenity). The dance forms follow the same hand gestures, or *hasta mudras,* for each of these *rasas*.

Abhinaya is one of the specialised aspects of dance and is considered the soul of the performance. The great queen of *abhinaya* is the late Balasaraswati, whose no two performances in Bharatanatyam were ever the same.

The genesis of contemporary styles of classical dance can be traced to the period between AD1300-1400. India offers a number of classical dance forms where each form embodies the influences of the region from which it originates. The links given below provide information about Indian dances as still practiced in India.

Bharatanatyam

Bharatanatyam is arguably the oldest and most traditional classical dance style which seemas a synthesis of philosophy, sculpture, music and literature. People generally hold the misconception that this dance style means Indian dance. This is not so. Possibly this dance got its name from Sage Bharata who wrote the **Natya Shastra.**

This dance originated in Tamil Nadu in south of India. Temples in south India abound in sculptures in shrines depicting celestial musicians and dancers, called *gandharvas* and *apsaras*. It seems dance and music were central to the lives of not only gods and goddesses, but also to those people who built the temples. Nataraja as the dancing Shiva is worshipped in Bharatanatyam as the God of dance.

Cultural historians attribute the dance form to have originated from the well-known figurine of a young female dancer from Mohenjodaro (ca 2300-1750 BC). Even the texts of the golden age of Tamil literature, known as Sangam Age, testify to the dance tradition flourishing at the time. Came the Pandavas, the Pandyas and the Hoysalas, who not only gave patronage to dance but also built temples with dancing figures carved in stone on pillars and *gopurams* (gateways). For centuries, dance was performed in temples by d*evadasis* or young girls as oblation at Gods feet.

Bharatanatyam is an energetic dance form wherein the postures are balanced positions, i.e. the weight of the body is placed squarely down the centre of the body. There is emphasis on the striking of the floor with the feet. There are jumps in the air as also pirouettes called *bhramaris*. There are movements done with the knees contacting the floor. These are called *mandi adavus*.

Bharatanatyam can be performed solo or in a group. The pure dance is called *nritta* and the expressive is *nritya*. The solo dancer uses various methods of story-telling to interpret the verses and stories she performs. The person who conducts the recital is called the *natatuvanar,* who is generally the guru of the dancer. He or she plays the cymbals called *nattuvangam.* The other musicians are the vocalist, the *mridangist* or percussion player, a flutist, a violinist and a *veena* player.

The items in a traditional presentation were composed and designed by four brothers who were known as the Tanjore Quartet. They were court musicians in the palace of Thanjavur and extremely talented. Their compositions are still in use by the dancers. The repertoire set by them was one variety of Carnatic musical forms as given below:

- *Alarippu* is a kind of warming up of the body before the actual dance performance. *Alarippu* is an invocation to God beginning with *anjali hasta* or *pushpanjali*. It has simple dance movements in which offering is made to God, the guru and to the audience. The conductor of the recital recites the mnemonics while playing the cymbals.

- *Jatiswaram* is an alteration of *sollukattu* (recitation) and *swara* (singing). The dance involves weaving of rhythmic patterns to interpret the melodic passages.

- *Shabdam* is based on a musical composition that extols a deity, essentially Lord Krishna or Lord Muruga by a description of his mighty deeds. The dancer now introduces the emotive aspect of the dance for the first time through thematic treatment with *abhinaya*.

- *Varnam* constitutes the central piece of the recital. The *varnam* combines pure dance with textual interpretation. The dancer's scholarship and artistic grasp over *abhinaya* is often judged by the *varnam*. *Varnam* with any stylised musical form and dance shows the *nayika* (female artist) expressing her love and devotion for the *nayaka* (male artist) who is a manifestation of the Almighty. It is a pure dance set to *mridangam* or drum syllables recited by the *nattuvanar*.

- *Padam* was first composed by Kshetrayya in the 17th century. The theme is romance with the lovelorn heroine dancing in various moods. It is usually in slow tempo to express the deeper emotions. Both the musician and dance synchronise their abilities to create *rasa*.

- *Jawali* is a dance piece set to verse. It is difficult to perform in the sense that its expression is faster. Here the lovelorn hero or heroine expresses his or her state of mind to the friend (*sakhi* or *sakha*). The song and dance are delivered in a middle tempo to convey a bit of humour. Lyrical compositions with the devotional theme, as the *keertanas* of Purandradasa, are often used as the base for the dance.

- *Kirtanam* is a lively composition that describes the dance of Shiva. It is a combination of movements and *abhinaya* or expression of the story.

- *Tillana* is performed towards the end of a Bharatanatyam recital. The dance is brisk in pace and has statuesque poses. It is a *nritta* item of verse full of rhythmic challenges. At times, the item ends with a short interpretative passage sung, sans rhythm occasionally and addressed to some deity.

- *Sloka* is in Sanskrit and is presented as the final item and sung in praise of or in prayer to God.

One of the greatest performers of Bharatanatyam has been Balasaraswati who was influential in popularising the dance as much as Rukmini Devi Arundale. Balasaraswati was famous for her soulful renderings of *abhinaya* or mimetic pieces, in which she not only danced but sang as well.

Kathak

Kathak, a predominant dance form of north India, derives its name from *katha* (story) since it originated from the devotional recitation by story-tellers or *kathakars*, who were attached to temples. The *kathakars* used to tell the story through music and dance. During the medieval period it received special patronage from both the Mughal and Hindu rulers.

The Kathak presentation is divided into three distinct parts: the *natya* (drama), the *nritta* (pure dance) and the *nritya* (expression, mimetic). While *nritta* is a logical extension of words and imagery of movements, inclusion of the *natya* to the dance gives it substance. *Nritya* combines dancing and acting while interpreting the story. In delineation of these aspects, the *rasa* or emotion charges the atmosphere radiating *ananda* (bliss) on union with God. Known for its intricate compositions, rapid *chakkars* or *bhramaris* (pirouettes), complex *tatkar* (footwork) and stylised facial expressions, Kathak hails from three *gharanas*—Banaras, Lucknow and Jaipur. While the Jaipur *gharana* focuses on *layakari* or rhythmic permutations, the Lucknow *gharana* expounds on *bhava* or moods and emotions with graceful movement and delicate placing of hands. This dance style was influenced by the Awadh royalty.

The costume of the Kathak dancer resembles the dress worn by figures in Mughal miniature paintings and the dance is performed by both men and women.

Inextricably tied to Hindustani music, the dance revolves around the Radha and Sri Krishna themes. The dancer dances with 200 *ghungroos* (bells on the feet) and the musical accompaniments are the *sarangi* and *tabla*. This dance form has gliding movements with no jerky or angular gestures. With a straight back, one arm is held vertically while the other is extended at shoulder height. While the body remains still, the dancer executes fast-paced dance steps. Traditionally a solo dance, it lends itself to group compositions too, as in *Rasleela* of Vrindaban which is an expression of operatic treatment. Items revolving around the themes of *nava-rasas* (nine moods) and the *ashta-nayikas* (eight states of maiden in love) are part of *abhinaya*.

The most well-known performers of Kathak today are Guru Birju Maharaj and Shovana Narain.

Kathakali

Kathakali is a stylised dance-drama from Kerala depicting the victory of truth over falsehood. *Katha* means a story and *kali* is a play. The roots of the dance form can be traced to about 1,500 years earlier. The dance-drama symbolises the blending of Aryan and Dravidian cultures and is presumed to have evolved from the tradition of the region like Krishnattam, Ramanattam, Kudiyattam, Mudayyetu and Theyyam.

The classical elements of Kathakali come from the Sanskrit theatre called Kudiyattam. There are four types of enactments—*angikan* or limb movements, *varhikam* or words, *aaharyam* or make-up and costumes, *satvikam* or emotional aspects. In Krishnattam and Ramanattam, Jayadeva's poem *Geeta-Govinda* is adopted for devotional singing. It was especially popular at the Guruvayoor temple dedicated to Sri Krishna. Theyyam is a ritualistic art form practiced in the village temple of Malabar area. The more vigorous dance patterns and exaggerated expressions found in Kathakali are adaptations from Theyyam.

Being a very exacting art, it demands strenuous training of the body and facial movements. Kathakali combines dance with dialogue to bring myth and legend to life in the temple courtyards of Kerala.

The origin of the dance can be traced to the middle of the 17th century. Like the other dance-dramas, the themes of Kathakali are drawn from the *Ramayana*, the *Mahabharata* and the *Bhagwata Purana*. Like Bharatanatyam, this dance form too is based on the *Natya Shastra*. Highly stylised and evolved, the traditional dance requires elaborate masks and costumes. The dancers wear huge skirts and head-dress and their make-up is very intricate, imparting the dance a weird and at the same time fantastic aspect. The accompaniments include the *chenda*, a drum like instrument that produces thunderous beats and the *maddala* that produces a softer sound, and two large cymbals.

Today's Kathakali is based on two styles—Kalladikodam and Kapplingadam. The first lays importance on rigorous training and stylised body movements. Emotions are expressed not through the face alone. Here the *natya dharmi* method is adopted. The hand gestures are wider and in conjunction with body movements.

Kathakali uses elaborate hand gestures and very formalised facial expressions. The latter has to be learnt and practiced at the feet of the *ashaan*. The male singers sing the *sahitya* or verses alternately. The dancer interprets the lyrics literally before creating a drama of fantasy around the words. He travels to other worlds—forests, mountains to *bhulokam*—the world of evil and to *swarga*—the world of gods. Mostly he goes to the inner world in himself where he exercises his imagination.

The late Chengannur Raman Pillai codified the dance and taught it in school to his disciples. P.V. Balakrishnan is an exponent of the ancient form of Kathakali.

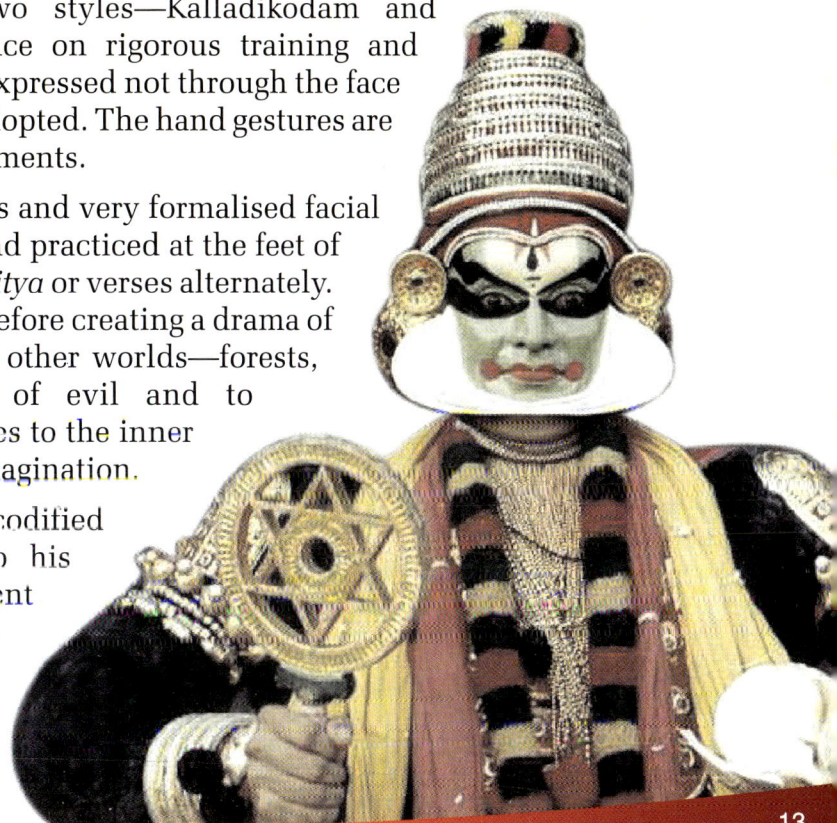

Manipuri

Manipuri is a traditional dance of Manipur in north-east of India. This dance form with its lyrical movements takes the mind on a peaceful journey. The people of the land were called Meithei and performed the ritual dance, the *jogoi* or circular dance, which is the precursor to present-day Manipuri. The Manipur tradition of worshiping their gods through dance and music was an integral part of the peoples life. One of the oldest rituals is called Lai Haraoba where the dance portrays the process of creation of the universe.

According to legend, Lord Shiva and Goddess Parvati are said to have danced in the valleys of Manipur and this tradition of dance continues till today.

Contrary to the convention of the later Hindu temples, *maibis* or the high priestess, and not the priests, conduct the ceremonial functions in temples. The greatest cultural evolution took place in the 18th century during the reign of King Bhagyachandra, one of the most enlightened kings, who was a devotee of Lord Vishnu. During his reign began the resurgence of arts in Manipur. He founded the *Rasleelas* and *Nat Sankirtana*. The art of *Sankirtana* involves singing and beating of the drum to narrate the story of Sri Krishna.

The male *Sankirtana* is called *nupapala* while the female is *nupipala*. The dancer is always male.

There are two dance forms in Manipur —*Pung cholom* or drum dance, and *Kartal cholom* or cymbal dance, where the performer plays a musical instrument or claps while dancing. The bent-knee position, with the torso, slightly bend forward is the basic stance. Majority of the movements, including various jumps and turns with complicated footwork, are carried out in this position. Some of the most exciting movements are mid-air rolling pirouettes while playing the instrument.

Rasleela forms the core of the classical tradition. There are different kinds of *Rasleelas* where Radha and Sri Krishna dance with the *gopis*. Every *Ras* is preceded with a *rupapala* or a male Sankirtana which serves the purpose of *purvaranga* or the prelude. Themes from *Geeta Purana, Bhagwata Purana* and compositions from the *Gita-Govinda* predominate the repertoire. The Radha-Krishna legend is frequently performed in Manipuri. As symbols of the female and male forces in Nature, their union and creation constitute the principal themes. The dance tradition recreates the life and deeds of Radha and Krishna.

The Manipuri dance lays emphasis on involving the entire body rather than the facial expressions. *Rasleela* lays emphasis on lyrical grace and delicacy of hand gestures. The different movements of the male and female dancers is very clean in Manipuri. The female dancer is very poised and gentle. The male dancer is powerful and energetic. Facial expression is minimal and movements are circular in form, flowing from one to another. The hands and wrists are used constantly. The costumes are very simple. Two young children usually play the role of Radha and Krishna. Women play the roles of the chief *sakhi* and *gopis*, all of whom wish to be united with Sri Krishna. This is called *shingara-bhakti* for God.

Guru Singhajit Singh and his wife-cum-disciple Charu Seja Mathur are versatile exponents of this dance form.

Kuchipudi

Kuchipudi, the dance-drama (referred to as *Ata Bhagavatham*) from Andhra Pradesh, is based on themes drawn from the Hindu epics, the *Ramayana* and the *Mahabharata*. It is a folk-dance style quite close to Bharatanatyam while retaining its folk origin. Kuchipudi has been the result of the Bhakti movement in the 6th century. In the 17th century, Siddendra Yogi, the progenitor of the form, presented a dance-drama with boys from the village of Kuchipudi. The techniques used then were passed on to the subsequent generations.

Kuchipudi plays are performed in the open air on an improvised stage at night. The *sutradhar,* or master of ceremonies, plays an integral role in introducing the characters, providing humour and tying together the show. The fast-paced nature of the form has made it a popular dramatic form. Today it is better known as a solo dance.

Kuchipudi costumes look similar to those worn in Bharatanatyam dance. Elegant footwork is an important aspect of Kuchipudi. Another distinctive aspect of this dance is that in special performances, the dance is executed on brass plates and moving the plate with the feet to the tune of the accompanying music. Yet another is the formation of beautiful floor patterns using efficient feet movements. The performer has to express through dance and gestures, the speech and song. The artiste, apart from being a dancer and actor, has to have a high proficiency in Sanskrit and Telugu languages, music and the texts for the performance.

The Kuchipudi performance begins with recital of extracts from the four *Vedas* as these symbolise the composition of the *Natyaveda.* This is followed by Ganapati *stuti* before the entry of the *sutradhar* who narrates the dance-drama with its implications and introduces the artistes. Each dancer is introduced with a *pravesa daruvu* or entrance number accompanied by song and rhythmic syllables. The word *daruvu* means rhythmic pattern. There is *nritta, nritya* and *natya.* The *nritta* part is composed of *teeermanams* and *jatis*; the *nritya* consists of *sabdams* introduced to enrich the dance and *natya* is acting with *mudras* to enact the stories of yore.

Kuchipudi classical dance comprises of a blend of the *tandava* and *lasya* elements. The music in this dance form is classical and the costumes are conventional. *Bhagavatula Ramayya,* written by Hari Madhavayya, introduced the dance-drama in the Kuchipudi repertoire; and today *vachikabhinaya* (verbal expression) has become a special feature of Kuchipudi dance-drama.

Vedantam Laxmi Narayana Sastry introduced solo items and laid the foundation of the Kuchipudi repertoire. Today Raja and Radha Reddy have taken this dance form to new heights.

Odissi

Odissi is a popular dance form of Orissa that lies on the eastern coast of India. This area is studded with caves and temples. The walls of Rani-Gumpha cave at Udayagiri are adorned with sculpture of a dancer accompanied by musicians performing in front of a king. It is assumed that the roots of this performing art had their genesis in 2nd century AD According to the local inhabitants, Lord Shiva and his son Ganesh taught dance to a beautiful *apsara* (dancer from heaven) called Manirambha. Shiva was found portrayed as Nataraja in the postures of *tandava* dance in Parasurameswar temple. They also believe that sometime between 2nd century BC and 2nd century AD Sage Bharata taught the dance to Sage Attahas, who taught it to the *maharis*—the temple dancers of Orissa or Odhradesh as it was called then. Poet Jayadeva wrote a beautiful Sanskrit poem called *Gita-Govinda*, that is about the love of Radha for Sri Krishna and her desire to be united with him. Radha became central during the Chaitanya era from 16th century onwards. The neo-Vaisnavism of this period created the right environment for development of the dance tradition.

The *maharis* lived as servants of the deity, Lord Jagannath and on support from the temple funds. *Maharis* were the only ones to be permitted into the inner shrine of the temple. Then there were the *nachunis* who danced in the royal court. Finally there were *gotipuas* or young boys who were trained in gymnastics and performed before the public. With the advent of British, the *maharis* faded out of the picture and the *nachunis* too disappeared. Only *gotipuas* survived and from them the Odissi dance style developed. Some artistes even revived the dying art of Odissi by looking at sculptures carved on walls of temples and by studying the treatise, *Abhinaya Chandrika*.

Odissi has emerged as a sculpturesque dance style in which the head, bust and torso move in soft flowing movements to express specific moods and emotions. The basic *chawka* position is a half-sitting posture used constantly by the dancer. The form is curvaceous, based on the *tribhang* or division of body into three parts—head, bust and torso. The *mudras* and expressions are similar to those of Bharatanatyam. The dance is replete with love for Sri Krishna, the eighth incarnation of Lord Vishnu.

Odissi is divided into *nritta* (pure dance) and *abhinaya* (expressional dance). In a classical Odissi performance, the invocatory dance is called *mangalacharan*. The dancer enters carrying flowers to place before the image of Lord Jagannath on the stage or the dancer can begin her performance with *bhoomi pranam*. Sanskrit *slokas* are recited in praise of Ganesh, Saraswati and Vishnu. *Mangalacharan* is performed with the hands joined in *anjali* in front of the heart in greeting. This includes movement in eight directions to cover the stage and concludes with *trikhandi pranam*, hands held aloft to the gods, the guru and the *rasikas* (the audience). The recital continues with *vatu nrittya*, which paints the entire gamut of Odissi *nritta*. The instruments used in Odissi are the *mardala* (drum), the *manjira* (cymbals), the flute and the violin. The dancer wears the typical Oriya sari and silver jewellery.

The legendary figure in Odissi dance is Guru Kelucharan Mohapatra, who with his disciple, the late Sanjukta Panigrahi contributed to the establishment of this style.

Mohiniattam

Mohiniattam is essentially a feminine dance of Kerala recorded to have begun between the 3rd and 8th century AD. Legend says that Lord Vishnu took the form of Mohini to entice the *asuras* (demons). During the churning of the ocean, the *asuras* rushed towards the bowl of nectar. Vishnu appeared in the feminine form of Mohini to entice the *asuras* and took the bowl away.

Literally meaning the dance of the enchantress, Mohiniyattam was mainly performed in the temple precincts of Kerala. This dance form found acceptance in the 16th century and in 19th century Maharaja Swati Tirunal of Travancore encouraged it. The most popular *padams* in Mohiniattam, composed by Swati Tirunal, describe the heroine's yearning for her lover. Lord Vishnu or Sri Krishna is more often the hero.

Mohiniattam was conceived as a form of social diversion. It is essentially a solo dance performed by women with tender and graceful body movements in the *lasya* style. Hand gestures play an important role as a communication system. The dominant emotion in this dance form is *shringara* or love for the Divine.

The dancer wears a white sari resplendent in a gold border. On festive occasions, young girls perform this dance in a circle with simple movements, while singing songs.

The repertoire of Mohiniattam follows closely that of Bharatanatyam. Mohiniattam, like other forms, follows the *Hasthalakshana Deepika* as textbook of hand gestures. The basic steps in this dance form are *adavus—toganam, jaganam, dhaganam* and *sammisram*. The *adavus* or steps are set to musical compositions. The *varnam* has a simple format with greater emphasis on *abhinaya* and less on *nritta* or pure dance.

The performance begins with Ganapati *stuti* or invocation followed by *mukhachalam*, a pure dance item in which the graceful delineation of characteristic movements is seen. The repertoire of Mohiniattam consists of five principal items, starting with *cholkettu*, then *varnam, jatiswaram, padam* and concluding with *tillana*. *Varnam* combines pure and expressional dance, while *padam* tests the histrionic talent of a dancer and *tillana* reveals her technical artistry. Jayadevas *Gita-Govinda* is most popularly performed to depict the divine love of Radha and Sri Krishna.

The most well-known performers of this dance are Ms Kanak Rele and Ms Bharati Shivaji.

Chhau or the mask-dance of Orissa in eastern India had its origin in the martial art form. The word *chhau* originates from the Sanskrit word *chhaya* or shade in reference to the mask that the dancer wears. While the Chhau dance of Bihar and West Bengal makes use of the mask during the dance, the Mayurbhanj Chhau does not use masks. It is performed traditionally by men and is related to the Shiva cult in Orissa. No dais or raised platform is required as the dance is performed on the ground and the audience sits around the performer.

It is essentially a tribal dance performed in the olden days to appease the Sun-god. In this form, the dancers use movements that require a high degree of control, balance and skill. One leg is raised to the level of the chest, rotating it around the body while the dancer stands balanced on the other leg. The Bihari Chhau is performed with pretty masks on and the dance is based on themes like the night, the moon, the sun and Nature. It is an extremely lyrical style of dance, almost feminine.

The West Bengal Chhau is performed with great vigour and with very elaborate masks and headgear. It is a very manly form of dance and entails leaps in the air, somersaults and twirls again and again. The dancers are male and require a strong stamina and control over technique. The actors play the roles of Ganesha, Durga, Shiva and other mythological characters. The prime objective of this dance is to show that evil forces are vanquished by righteous forces.

The accompanying music is based on Hindustani *raga* and instruments like *dhol*, drums and *shehnai* provide vigour to the dance movements.

Andhra Natyam

Andhra Natyam is a classical dance form from Andhra Pradesh, a state in South India. This traditional dance form originated as a temple dance dating back to as early as 2,000 years. It is a dance form that got lost in the Mughal period and the British days, but somehow came to be revived in the 20th century.

It is derived from a number of dance forms and has strong similarities to Kuchipudi and Bharatanatyam, including the older dance styles lie Dasiattam, Kacheriattam and Chinnamelam. Besides temple dancing, court dances by courtesans known as *kalavantulu* and open-air performances for the public, known as *kalapam* are also included under the category of Andhra Natyam.

It is a dance performed essentially by female dancers and is characterised by a rich display of footwork and superior *abhinaya*. Unlike the original version, the present Andhra Natyam is performed in stylish costumes, bold make-up, bright ornaments and to the an accompaniment of an orchestra. The musical instruments used as accompaniment include the *mridangam*, *manjira*, *veena*, the violin, *venu*, *tanpura*, *surpeti* and the *kanjira*.

Folk Dances of India

An Introduction:

Indian folk dances are performed to express joy. The folk dances are extremely simple with minimum of steps or movements. They are full of verve and vitality. Folk dances are performed for every possible occasion, to celebrate the arrival of seasons, birth of a child, weddings and festivals. Men and women perform some dances separately, while in some performances men and women dance together. On most occasions, the dancers sing themselves, while being accompanied by artists on the instruments. Each form of dance has a specific costume. The northeastern part of the country is the home to over 60 tribes. Each tribe has its own range of tribal dances. Most of these astonishing dances are performed to celebrate spring and harvest. In the south, the dummy horse dance or the *Poikalkuthirai*, is very famous. Dancers fit dummy legs to their legs and dance to the tune of music. Both men and women perform this form of art. In west, most of the dancers place a number of pots or *matkas* on their heads and dance while balancing them.

India can boast of an innumerable number of folk dances, each forming a speciality of a particular region or tribe. Each form has its own attraction and grace.

These dances have specific costumes and most costumes are flamboyant with elaborate jewels. The various dance forms have also developed a particular form of make-up for the performance, which is a skill by itself. Several dance schools today incorporate costume designing and make-up as special sections of the curriculum. The costumes for all forms are elaborate and rich. Flowers adorn their hair and in case of portrayal of gods, their necks are garlanded. The hall is also richly decorated with flowers. Application of mehandi *(henna)* in various styles is also an essential part of the make-up in most forms.

While there are numerous folk and tribal dances, there is constantly improvement. The skill and the imagination of the dancers influence the performance.

Folk in common parlance today indicates community and expressions that are spontaneous. It can vary from village to village but they all share a common heritage of myths and symbols. Their expressions reflect their geographical positioning and relationship to Nature. In the following pages, some of the prominent folk dances have been described in brief.

Bhangra (Punjab)

Bhangra is a popular dance of Punjab, a state in north India. Shouts of "*Hoye, balle….balle….*" are the magic words that can send any Punjabi into rapture. There is no other dance than Bhangra, the pride of Punjab, which castes its spell on the dancer and the viewer alike with such an impact. Bhangra, if not the most robust, is one of India's popular folk-dances. The festival of Baisakhi, family gatherings and get-togethers are some occasions for performing a quick Bhangra number. This dance, with its accompaniments and songs on *dholak* (drum), is never performed for religious purpose.

Bhangra is an energetic, all male, harvest dance which is instantly recognisable by the traditional head-dress and the vigorous arm movements. The dancers snap their fingers, do balancing tricks and indulge in acrobatic feats. They recite witty couplets known as *bolis* which may be just sheer exuberance, or may mouth meaningless sounds, such as "*Hoay, hoay*". The beats on the *dholak* prod the dancer to perform with greater vigour and indulge in light-hearted banter and satire in the couplets. Colourful clothes comprise of flowing turbans, *chadra* (cloth sheets covering for the lower body) and long *kurtas* (shirts) and waistcoats making this dance a treat to watch.

The counterpart of the Bhangra is the **Gidda**, which is gentler and is danced by the women-folk of Punjab. They dance in a collective number, but very often individual dancers or pairs detach themselves from the group to perform while the rest keep clapping in rhythm. The *dholki* (drum) provides the musical beats and often singers maintain the beat by tapping spoons on the body of the drum while the women mouth *boliyan* (couplets). They don colourful *salwar kameez* which is their regional dress. The dancers of Bhangra and Gidda need an inborn sense of rhythm, and which cannot be acquired easily.

Bihu (Assam)

Bihu is the most popular folk-dance of Assam and is enjoyed by all, be they young or old. Bihu is celebrated to mark the beginning of the spring festival, sometime in mid April. This festival is called the **Rongali Bihu**. Essentially a festival meant to celebrate the agricultural season, it is celebrated through Bihu dance accompanied by wild and lusty beats of the *dhol* (drum), *pepa* (buffalo hornpipe), *gogona* (a string reed attached to a bamboo piece at the end), *takka* (a portion of bamboo split to form a clapper) and Bihu songs woven round the theme of love. The most common formation in this dance is the circle or parallel rows. The Bihu dance demonstrates, through song and dance, the soul of the Assamese at its richest. The festival and the dance continue for about a month.

Except for Bhangra, no other folk dance in India can compete with the rhythmic exuberance of Bihu. This dance is performed by young boys and girls, who dance together, but there is no mixing of the sexes. The dance is characterised by brisk stepping, flinging and flipping of hands and swaying of hips representing youthful passion, reproductive urge and *joie de vivre*.

A tourist on a visit to Assam, during the harvest season, can witness the Bihu dance in almost every nook and corner of the Brahmaputra valley. Numerous organisations in Assam arrange *sammelans* (meets) where the people congregate to discuss various issues.

Lavani (MahaRaashtra)

Lavani is a folk dance of MahaRaashtra, a state in west India. Riding on a strong pro-MahaRaashtrian cultural wave, it is this dance form which is very popular among the Marathi speaking people. The history of the *tamasha* (drama) tradition of MahaRaashtra presents a picture that is somewhat different from the other folk forms. *Tamasha* is another name for the Lavani performance.

A gorgeous *mulgi* (woman) dressed in a *navwari* (a nine-yard sari) with a dazzling border and a *gajra* (bunch of flowers) in full bloom adorning her hair, looking *assal* (real) MahaRaashtrian, is seen swaying and swirling to the remix of *Disla ga bai disla*. This is one of the art forms which has stood the test of time and has been rediscovered of late.

Lavani has been rejuvenated and many Lavani shows are organised these days, both on the stage and the screen. People love to watch the sensuous Lavani dance movements and gestures in plush auditoriums too, where the dancers, dressed in extravagant costumes and against lavish sets, dance vigorously. Here the dance needs no *vag*, the drama part of *tamasha* from where Lavani originates.

This age-old folk dance is understood and appreciated by all, and not by the MahaRaashtrians alone. This dance is famous for its sex appeal and rules the hearts of the people, particularly of those living in the rural areas where other sources of entertainment are limited.

Dandiya Raas (Gujarat)

Dandiya Raas is a very popular folk dance of Gujarat which is nowadays danced in every nook and corner of other parts of India too. *"Kem cho? Majama che!"* is as famous as the dance itself, showing the spirit of camaraderie that the *Gujjus* (the Gujaratis) share with others. Dandiya Raas is the most ancient dance of Gujarat and is popular among the urban and the rural folk alike.

Like other dances, this dance also traces back its roots to Indian mythology. Radha's love for Sri Krishna has become immortal, and is often portrayed in various forms of dance, particularly with Krishna playing with the *gopis*. This folk dance, known as Raas, originated approximately 5,000 years ago. The performance is an all-time favourite dance of Gujaratis. It is usually performed during the festival of Navaratri.

Dandiya Raas is a simple, rhythmic dance performed by young people moving around in imaginary circles with measured steps to the beat of two *dandiya* (sticks) that each dancer carries in his or her hands. The beat for the dance is kept by striking the two sticks with each other in one's hands and sometimes with the sticks of the other dancer. The beat can even be maintained by clapping the hands. Ideally a circle of men move in either a clockwise direction while the circle of women move in an anti-clockwise direction or vice versa. The songs sung as an accompaniment are essentially amorous.

Dandiya Raas is a very energetic, colourful and playful dance providing a good opportunity to the young men and women for acting and exchanging messages through eye contact.

Garba (Gujarat)

Garba, another dance by women of Gujarat, is performed, in honour of Goddess Amba. This fertility dance begins by placing perforated earthen pots with oil lamps inside to the pots symbolise the embryonic life. Each pot is then balanced on every dancer's head as she and the others move around in circles, snapping their fingers and clapping their hands to produce a fast beat.

At times even men dance the Garba while singing and clapping like the by womenfolk, and this form of dance is known as **Garbi**. Traditionally the Garba is danced only at night. In an evolved version, the dance can be performed for its own sake and at any time. It is thus especially performed on occasions of weddings, festivals, engagements and other moments of happiness.

Ghoomar (Rajasthan)

Ghoomar is an elegant, whirling dance of the Rajputs who hail from Rajasthan. The dance is traditionally a performance by women in the Maharaja's court for celebrating Gauri *puja*. Women dance together in front of a statue of Lord Shiva and his consort Parvati within the *haveli*, far from the peering eyes of menfolk. Today it is a popular folk dance performed at weddings and festivals, and often danced into the late hours of the night.

The swaying movements of the women are enhanced by the brightly coloured veils and flaring skirts as the women twirl in circles, both in clockwise and in anti-clockwise directions. This is an elegant group dance employing beautiful hand gestures and gentle hip movements.

Ghoomar dancers dress traditionally in colourful Rajasthani skirts when dancing. The dance is performed to the accompaniment of musical instruments like the *dholak* and the *pakhawaj*. At times, the dancers themselves sing the songs and at others, a group of singers sing to provide the musical background to the dance. The name *ghoomar* signifies turning round and making circles wearing the long *ghoomar lehengas*! Now, Ghoomar is performed with songs of valour and victory on festivals like Holi, Gangaur *puja*, Teej, etc.

Jatra & Baul are very popular forms of folk theatre for the Bengali-speaking people. In the early and mid 19th century, amateurs formed their own Jatra troupes and selected secular rather than religious themes to perform. The performances were centred on religious aspects and were highly melodramatic. Songs were sung as an accompaniment. They continue to be highly stylised forms of presentation characterised by songs sung by singer-actors who need no microphones. Songs mark the beginning or the closure of the scenes.

Baul is one of the few widely known forms of folk music in Bengal. The Baul singers are called Bauls themselves and the songs they sing are described as *Baul-gan*. It is a form of folk-cum-devotional singing in Bengal and the singers sing and dance with an *ektara* (a single-stringed instrument).

The Baul costume consists of a half-*dhoti* and saffron robes. Another noticeable feature of Baul is their hairstyle. The singer wears a necklace made of beads formed from the stems of *tulsi* (basil plant).

Earthen pot is an eminent symbol in Indian folk dances

Among the three Bs of Bengali folk music—Baul, Bhaoyaiya and Bhatiayali—Baul is distinguished from the others by its religious music and dance.

Vrita is yet another traditional folk dance of Bengal. This is a dance of invocation performed by childless women who worship God after their wish is fulfilled. At times, this

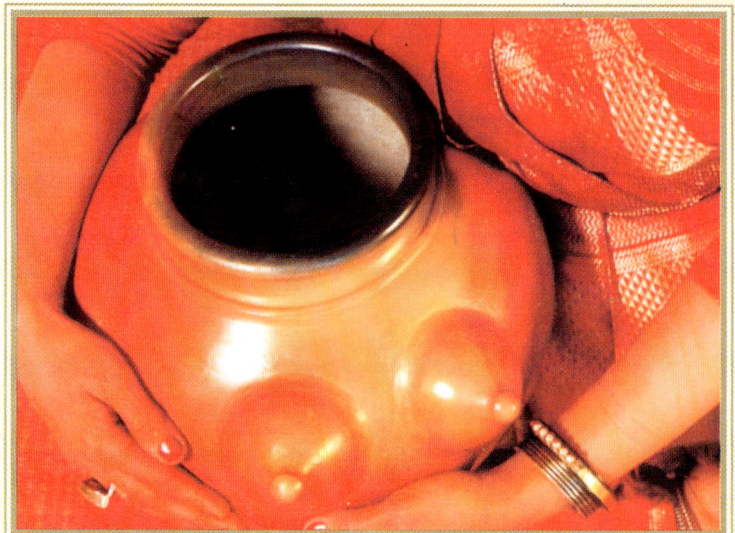

dance is performed on recovery from a serious illness.

Somewhat similar is the Kali *nach* performed during Gajan, in praise of Goddess Kali. The performers wear a mask after it has been blessed through recitation of *mantRaas* and the dancers dance with swords in their hands. This is essentially a male dance.

Dhamal Dance (Haryana)

Dhamal is a group dance and is as old as the era of *Mahabharata*. It is particularly in vogue in Mahendragarh and Jhajjar. The dance, rooted in the deeper emotions of the people, is performed on moonlit nights. When the winter veil of fog and mist lifts from the face of the earth and spring is in the air, the dancers assemble in an open space to stand in a circle. They start with a song to the sound of Dhamal beats. The songs sung during the dance relate to the burden of love and labour. They depict the villagers' hopes, aspirations, their love and their longings, their joys and sorrows. At least twenty dancers participate in the dance. Old musical instruments like the *sarangi, been, dholak* and the *khartals* constitute the orchestra.

Cheraw (Mizoram)

Cheraw is a very old and traditional dance of the Mizos which originated in the 1st century AD. This is also the most popular and colourful dance of the inhabitants of Mizoram. Long pairs of horizontal bamboo staves are tapped open and close in rhythmic beats by male members, who sit face to face on the ground. Girls, in colourful costumes of Puanchei, Kawrchei, Vakiria and Thihna, dance in and out between the beats of the bamboo. This dance is performed on almost all festive occasions. As bamboos are used for the dance, people sometimes call it the 'bamboo dance' too.

Gongs and drums are used to accompany the dance, but nowadays modern music is played to complement the dance.

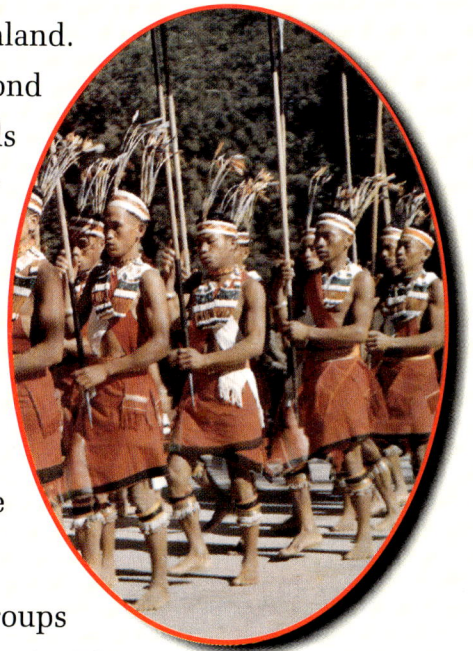

Naga dance is a popular dance of the tribals of Nagaland. The Nagas, blessed with high cheekbones, almond eyes, sparkling teeth, carrying bronze shields sheathed in bear skin and decorated spears, perform their dance with vigour.

All the Naga tribes have their particular harvest dances, though the most common is the Naga dance. The characteristic feature of the Naga dance is that the dancer dances in an erect posture with movements of the legs. There is a marked restricted use of the torso and the shoulders.

Another dance, the **Khamba Lim** is performed by two groups of men and women who stand in two rows. This gives us an insight into the inborn reticence of these people. War dances and other dances belonging to distinctive tribes constitute a major art form of Nagaland. In colourful costumes and jewellery, the dancers go through an amazing set of mock-war motions that could prove very dangerous, if one is a little careless. Festivals, marriages, harvests, or other moments of joy are occasions for the Nagas to burst into dance. And a sense of fun and frolic pervades the atmosphere when the Nagas dance.

Dhumal (Kashmir)

Dhumal is a dance performed by the menfolk of the Wattal tribe of Kashmir on festive occasions. The performers wear long colourful robes and tall conical caps that are studded with beads and shells. They move in a procession carrying a banner in a very ceremonial fashion. The banner is dug into the ground and the men begin to dance, forming a circle The musical backgound is provided by a drummer and vocal singing is by the participants.

Dhumal is performed on set occasions and at set locations. The drum is used as the accompanying instrument. The costumes for the dancers are akin to those for the Bhangra dancer of Punjab. This dance represents the 'never-say-die' spirit of the Kashmiris.

Another dance performed on festive occasions by the Kashmiris is **Rouff,** which is also a folk dance of this state in north India. It is danced solely by Kashmiri women who display their aptitude in performing simple footwork, while joining hands with each other and dancing in unison.

Singhi Chham (Sikkim)

Singhi Chham is a mask dance of Sikkim, depicting the snow-lion, which is the cultural symbol of the state. The third highest mountain in the world, the Kanchenjunga, stands as the sentinel over the Sikkim state and is believed to resemble the legendary snow-lion. The natives display their cultural symbol by dressing up in furry costumes and performing this majestic mask dance.

People use this imposing dance as a way to display their cultural symbol. Performed exclusively by citizens of the state, the dance is performed solely by menfolk in the month of September. The dancers are dressed up in esoteric masks, flashing silks, opulent brocades and embroidered boots.

Taranghmel (Goa)

Taranghmel is a multi-hued dance performed with all energy and youthfulness. On the occasions of Dussehra and Holi, young spirited girls and boys swarm the streets of Goa in colourful groups, waving flags and *tarang* (streamers), inspiring and inviting one and all to join in the festivities. They shout, "Ho! Ho!" to the beats of *romut, dhol* and *tasha*. The rainbow-like costumes of the dancers and the multi-coloured flags and streamers make the Taranghmel dance a visually appealing affair.

Dollu Kunitha is a popular drum-dance of Karnataka. The vigorous drum-dance is performed by the male members of the shepherd community, known as Kourba. Powerful and loud drum beats, acrobatic movements and attractive formations are the main highlights of the dance. Carrying large drums, decorated with coloured clothes and slung from their necks, the men beat the drums as they dance with nimble movements of the feet and legs. The dance is, at times, accompanied by songs, which are either religious or in praise of war.

Kinnauri Nati (Himachal Pradesh)

Kinnauri Nati is a dance of the people from the hills of Himachal Pradesh in the north. The pristine beauty of hilly Himachal finds an eloquent expression in the languid and elegant movements of Nati dancer. The dance matches the gentleness of the cool hilly breeze and the rhythmic swaying of trees. It is mainly a mime-dance and the most important Lati dance is Losar Shona Chuksom, which derives its name from Losai (new year). The dance movements depict all the activities involved in sowing and reaping the crops grown in the hills.

Hikat is another dance performed by women from Himachal. Forming pairs, the dancers extend their arms to the front, grip each other's waists and with bodies inclined back, go round and round on the same spot.

Nicobarese Dance (Andaman and Nicobar)

Nicobarese dance is the dance of the Nicobarese tribals who reside in the islands of Car Nicobar. The dance is performed during the Ossuary Feast or the Pig Festival. Dedicated to the departed head of the family, the occasion is observed with night-long dancing in full moonlight under the swaying palms dotting the island. The dancers dressed in coconut fronds, step gracefully in time to traditional songs. Feasting on island delicacies followed by a pig fight in the morning are the other attractions of the celebration.

Kudiyattam (Kerala)

Kudiyattam, a Sanskrit drama performed in Kerala, has been recognised by UNESCO as a Human Heritage Art. Rightly so. It is the oldest existing classical theatre form in the entire world, having originated much before Kathakali and most other theatrical forms.

Practised and preserved by the Chakyar community in Kerala, Kudiyattam is the oldest surviving link with ancient Sanskrit theatre. The stylised mode of acting, the same character playing different roles, the use of the spoken words into chanting, stories within stories, flash-backs, improvisations, eye expressions, an extensive gesture vocabulary, body movements and facial expressions, the use of Sanskrit by the main character and Malayalam by the court jester or *vidushaka*, who comments, satirizes and ridicules the protagonists, are the salient features of Kudiyattam.

Performances are traditionally held in the *koothambalam* which are special theatres attached to temples. The Sanskrit play selected for the performance usually takes over several days. Female dancers, called *nangiars*, deliver the invocatory songs and also participate. The use of the *tiRaashila* or curtain, different colours for the face to depict characters and elaborate ornaments are all similar to Kathakali. The *mizhavu* is a special drum used as an accompaniment for *Kudivattam* performances. The repertoire consists of most of the Sanskrit dramas like *Soorpanakhangam Kudiyattam* and *Jatayuvadham Kudivattam* from based on the Indian epics.

Common Props in Indian Dance

MATKAS (decorated pots):
Matkas only add color to the attire of the dancers. They have been the inspiration and an object of fascination behind many dances. These signify the dances from all parts of the country especially western states. Dancers put such 7-8 beautifully decorated colourful matkas on their heads & dance balancing them.

BAMBOO STICKS :
Who doesn't like to play with bamboo sticks? But dancing with them does sure guarantee more fun. Whether it Mizo dance from east or Bhangra from North, dancers display their breath-taking skills with this prop as no other dance in the world does!

DUPATTAS (Scarves) :
These pieces of cloth are symbolic to the different colors representing the spirit of dance altogether. Some tie it on the tip of their index fingers & dance and some place it around neck where as others dance with the cloth widespread. These are basically used to celebrate the time of spring & harvest.

DANDIYAS :
Dandiyas are again beautifully decorated colorful (much smaller than bamboo) sticks used in the most popular 'dandiya' dance of Gujarat.
Girls and boys go playing with these sticks during the dance, in a formation of circles, dancing clockwise & anticlockwise respectively. The sound of the striking of these sticks with one another are in the tune with the dandiya songs/beats.

MASKS :
Different Masks represent different moods of human beings (like Red represents Anger) and to a large extent also convey the message and meaning of a dance. These masks are generally used in South Indian Classical dances like Kudiyattom in which dancers use different masks to elaborate their dance. The characters who do not use the masks have specific facial colors applied to their face.

GHUNGROOS (Ringing anklets):
Any classical dancer is just incomplete without 'Ghungroos' tied to his/her ankle. The famous tapping dances of India are based on the lilting rhythms of the Ghungroos which combine and transcend one into the another and produce a magical effect.

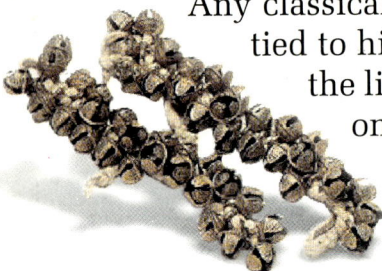